When it's time to take Baby bye-bye, tiny throws are just right for making car seats cozy and warm. Light weight yarn gives good definition to the dense stitches.

LEISURE ARTS, INC. • Maumelle, Arkansas

Cables

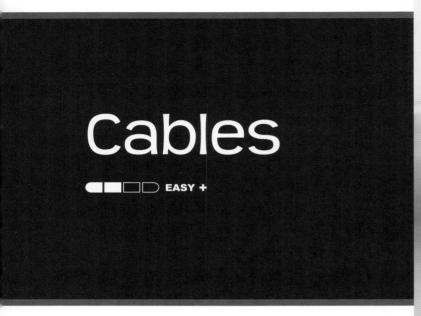

EASY +

Finished Size: 33" x 36½"
 (84 cm x 92.5 cm)

SHOPPING LIST

Yarn (Light Weight)
[3.5 ounces, 254 yards
(100 grams, 232 meters) per skein]:
☐ 6 skeins

Crochet Hook
☐ Size I (5.5 mm)
 or size needed for gauge

Additional Supplies
☐ Tapestry needle
☐ ¹³/₁₆" (20 mm) Buttons - 2

GAUGE INFORMATION

In pattern,

    one repeat (10 sts) = 3" (7.5 cm);

    8 rows = 3¼" (8.25 cm)

Gauge Swatch: 5½" wide x 4" high

    (14 cm x 10 cm)

Ch 19.

Work same as Body for 10 rows:

18 hdc.

Finish off.

BODY

Ch 109.

Row 1 (Right side)**:** Hdc in third ch from hook **(2 skipped chs count as first hdc, now and throughout)** and in each ch across: 108 hdc.

Note: Loop a short piece of yarn around any stitch to mark Row 1 as **right** side **and** bottom edge.

Row 2: Ch 2 **(counts as first hdc, now and throughout)**, turn; hdc in next hdc and in each hdc across.

Row 3: Ch 2, turn; hdc in next hdc, skip next 2 hdc 2 rows **below**, work FPdtr around each of next 2 hdc 2 rows **below**, working in **front** of last 2 FPdtr made, work FPdtr around each of 2 skipped hdc, hdc in next 2 hdc, ★ work FPtr around each of next 2 hdc 2 rows **below**, hdc in next 2 hdc, skip next 2 hdc 2 rows **below**, work FPdtr around each of next 2 hdc 2 rows **below**, working in **front** of last 2 FPdtr made, work FPdtr around each of 2 skipped hdc, hdc in next 2 hdc; repeat from ★ across.

Row 4: Ch 2, turn; hdc in next st and in each st across.

Row 5: Ch 2, turn; hdc in next hdc, work FPtr around each of next 4 FPdtr 2 rows **below**, hdc in next 2 hdc, ★ work FPtr around each of next 2 FPtr 2 rows **below**, hdc in next 2 hdc, work FPtr around each of next 4 FPdtr 2 rows **below**, hdc in next 2 hdc; repeat from ★ across.

Row 6: Ch 2, turn; hdc in next st and in each st across.

Row 7: Ch 2, turn; hdc in next hdc, skip next 2 FPtr 2 rows **below**, work FPdtr around each of next 2 FPtr 2 rows **below**, working in **front** of last 2 FPdtr made, work FPdtr around each of 2 skipped FPtr, hdc in next 2 hdc, ★ work FPtr around each of next 2 FPtr 2 rows **below**, hdc in next 2 hdc, skip next 2 FPtr 2 rows **below**, work FPdtr around each of next 2 FPtr 2 rows **below**, working in **front** of last 2 FPdtr made, work FPdtr around each of 2 skipped FPtr, hdc in next 2 hdc; repeat from ★ across.

Repeat Rows 4-7 for pattern until piece measures approximately 36" (91.5 cm) from beginning ch, ending by working a **right** side row; do **not** finish off.

EDGING

Rnd 1: Ch 1, do **not** turn; sc evenly around entire Body working 3 sc in each corner; join with slip st to first sc.

Rnd 2: Ch 1; working from **left** to **right**, work reverse sc in each sc around *(Figs. 3a-d, page 30)*; join with slip st to first st, finish off.

BUTTONHOLE STRAP (Make 2)
Ch 11.

Row 1 (Right side)**:** Working in back ridge of beginning ch *(Fig. 1, page 30)*, hdc in third ch from hook and each ch across: 10 hdc.

Row 2: Ch 2, turn; hdc in next hdc and in each hdc across.

Row 3 (Buttonhole row)**:** Ch 2, turn; hdc in next 3 hdc, ch 2, skip next 2 hdc, hdc in last 4 hdc: 8 hdc and one ch-2 sp.

Row 4: Ch 2, turn; hdc in next 3 hdc, 2 hdc in next ch-2 sp, hdc in last 4 hdc: 10 hdc.

Row 5: Ch 2, turn; hdc in next hdc and in each hdc across.

Repeat Row 5 until Strap measures approximately 7" (18 cm) from beginning ch.

Finish off leaving a long end for sewing.

Sew last row of each Strap approximately 8" (20.5 cm) from top edge of Body and 11" (28 cm) from each side edge. Sew buttons to Body, 12" (30.5 cm) from top edge and centered with each Strap.

Heirloom

◼◼◼◻ INTERMEDIATE

Finished Size: 38½" x 44½"
 (98 cm x 113 cm)

SHOPPING LIST

Yarn (Light Weight) 🧶3
[3.5 ounces, 254 yards
(100 grams, 232 meters) per skein]:
☐ 8 skeins

Crochet Hook
☐ Size I (5.5 mm)
    or size needed for gauge

Additional Supplies
☐ Tapestry needle

GAUGE INFORMATION

14 hdc and 9 rows = 4" (10 cm)

Gauge Swatch: 4" (10 cm) square

Ch 15.

Row 1: Hdc in third ch from hook **(2 skipped chs count as first hdc)** and in each ch across: 14 hdc.

Rows 2-9: Ch 2 **(counts as first hdc)**, turn; hdc in next hdc and in each hdc across.

Finish off.

STITCH GUIDE

BACK POST DOUBLE CROCHET
(abbreviated BPdc)

YO, insert hook from **back** to **front** around post of st indicated **(Fig. 2, page 30)**, YO and pull up a loop (3 loops on hook), (YO and draw through 2 loops on hook) twice.

FRONT POST DOUBLE CROCHET
(abbreviated FPdc)

YO, insert hook from **front** to **back** around post of st indicated **(Fig. 2, page 30)**, YO and pull up a loop (3 loops on hook), (YO and draw through 2 loops on hook) twice.

FRONT POST TREBLE CROCHET
(abbreviated FPtr)

YO twice, insert hook from **front** to **back** around post of st indicated **(Fig. 2, page 30)**, YO and pull up a loop even with loops on hook (4 loops on hook), (YO and draw through 2 loops on hook) 3 times. Skip hdc **behind** FPtr.

FRONT POST DOUBLE TREBLE CROCHET **(abbreviated FPdtr)**

YO 3 times, insert hook from **front** to **back** around post of st indicated **(Fig. 2, page 30)**, YO and pull up a loop even with loops on hook (5 loops on hook), (YO and draw through 2 loops on hook) 4 times. Skip hdc **behind** FPdtr.

POPCORN (uses one hdc)

5 Dc in hdc indicated, drop loop from hook, insert hook in first dc of 5-dc group, hook dropped loop and draw through dc.

WOVEN LATTICE PANEL
(Make 4)

Finished Size: 6" wide x 21" high (15 cm x 53.5 cm)

Ch 22.

Row 1 (Right side)**:** Hdc in third ch from hook (**2 skipped chs count as first hdc, now and throughout**) and in each ch across: 21 hdc.

Note: Loop a short piece of yarn around any stitch to mark Row 1 as **right** side **and** bottom edge.

Row 2: Ch 2 (**counts as first hdc, now and throughout**), turn; hdc in next hdc and in each hdc across.

Row 3: Ch 2, turn; hdc in next hdc, work FPtr around each of next 2 hdc 2 rows **below**, ★ hdc in next hdc, work FPtr around each of next 2 hdc 2 rows **below**; repeat from ★ across to last 2 hdc, hdc in last 2 hdc.

Row 4: Ch 2, turn; hdc in next st and in each st across.

Row 5: Ch 2, turn; hdc in next hdc, skip next 2 FPsts 2 rows **below**, work FPdtr around each of next 2 FPsts, hdc in next hdc, working in **front** of last 2 FPdtr made, work FPdtr around each of 2 skipped FPsts 2 rows **below**, ★ hdc in next hdc, skip next 2 FPsts 2 rows **below**, work FPdtr around each of next 2 FPsts, hdc in next hdc, working in **front** of last 2 FPdtr made, work FPdtr around each of 2 skipped FPsts 2 rows **below**; repeat from ★ once **more**, hdc in last 2 hdc.

Row 6: Ch 2, turn; hdc in next st and in each st across.

Row 7: Ch 2, turn; hdc in next hdc, work FPtr around each of next 2 FPdtr 2 rows **below**, hdc in next hdc, ★ skip next 2 FPdtr 2 rows **below**, work FPdtr around each of next 2 FPdtr, hdc in next hdc, working **behind** last 2 FPdtr made, work FPdtr around each of 2 skipped FPdtr 2 rows **below**, hdc in next hdc; repeat from ★ once **more**, work FPtr around each of next 2 FPdtr 2 rows **below**, hdc in last 2 hdc.

Rows 8-46: Repeat Rows 4-7, 9 times; then repeat Row 4-6 once **more**.

Row 47: Ch 2, turn; ★ hdc in next hdc, work FPtr around each of next 2 FPdtr 2 rows **below**; repeat from ★ across to last 2 hdc, hdc in last 2 hdc; finish off.

BASKETWEAVE BLOCK
(Make 4)

Finished Size: 8" (20.5 cm) square

Ch 30.

Row 1 (Right side)**:** Dc in fourth ch from hook (**3 skipped chs count as first dc**) and in each ch across: 28 dc.

Note: Mark Row 1 as **right** side **and** bottom edge.

Row 2: Ch 2, turn; work BPdc around each of next 2 dc, ★ work FPdc around each of next 2 dc, work BPdc around each of next 2 dc; repeat from ★ across to last dc, hdc in last dc.

Rows 3 and 4: Ch 2, turn; work FPdc around each of next 2 sts, ★ work BPdc around each of next 2 sts, work FPdc around each of next 2 sts; repeat from ★ across to last hdc, hdc in last hdc.

Rows 5 and 6: Ch 2, turn; work BPdc around each of next 2 sts, ★ work FPdc around each of next 2 sts, work BPdc around each of next 2 sts; repeat from ★ across to last hdc, hdc in last hdc.

Rows 7-18: Repeat Rows 3-6, 3 times.

Finish off.

BRAID PANEL (Make 4)

Finished Size: 4" wide x 8" high (10 cm x 20.5 cm)

Ch 15.

Row 1 (Right side)**:** Hdc in third ch from hook and in next ch, dc in next 2 chs, (hdc in next ch, dc in next 2 chs) twice, hdc in last 3 chs: 14 sts.

Note: Mark Row 1 as **right** side **and** bottom edge.

Row 2: Ch 2, turn; hdc in next st and in each st across.

Row 3: Ch 2, turn; hdc in next 2 hdc, skip next 3 sts 2 rows **below**, work FPdtr around each of next 2 dc 2 rows **below**, hdc in next hdc, working in **front** of last 2 FPdtr made, work FPdtr around each of first 2 skipped sts 2 rows **below**, hdc in next hdc, work FPtr around each of next 2 dc 2 rows **below**, hdc in last 3 hdc.

Row 4: Ch 2, turn; hdc in next st and in each st across.

Row 5: Ch 2, turn; hdc in next 2 hdc, work FPtr around each of next 2 FPdtr 2 rows **below**, hdc in next hdc, skip next 2 FPdtr 2 rows **below**, work FPdtr around each of next 2 FPtr, hdc in next hdc, working **behind** last 2 FPdtr made, work FPdtr around each of 2 skipped FPdtr 2 rows **below**, hdc in last 3 hdc.

Row 6: Ch 2, turn; hdc in next st and in each st across.

Row 7: Ch 2, turn; hdc in next 2 hdc, skip next 2 FPtr 2 rows **below**, work FPdtr around each of next 2 FPdtr, hdc in next hdc, working in **front** of last 2 FPdtr made, work FPdtr around each of 2 skipped FPtr 2 rows **below**, hdc in next hdc, work FPtr around each of next 2 FPdtr 2 rows **below**, hdc in last 3 hdc.

Rows 8-18: Repeat Rows 4-7 twice, then repeat Rows 4-6 once **more**.

Finish off.

HERRINGBONE PANEL
(Make 4)
Finished Size: 2½" wide x 13" high
(6 cm x 33 cm)

Ch 9.

Row 1 (Right side)**:** Hdc in third ch from hook and in each ch across: 8 hdc.

Note: Mark Row 1 as **right** side **and** bottom edge.

Row 2: Ch 2, turn; hdc in next hdc and in each hdc across.

Row 3: Ch 2, turn; work FPdtr around fourth st 2 rows **below**, hdc in next 4 hdc, work FPdtr around fifth st 2 rows **below**, hdc in last hdc.

Rows 4-29: Repeat Rows 2 and 3, 13 times.

Finish off.

POPCORN PANEL
(Make 4)
Finished Size: 9½" wide x 13" high
(24 cm x 33 cm)

Ch 34.

Row 1: Hdc in third ch from hook and in each ch across: 33 hdc.

Row 2 (Right side)**:** Ch 2, turn; hdc in next hdc, work Popcorn in next hdc, (hdc in next 3 hdc, work Popcorn in next hdc) across to last 2 hdc, hdc in last 2 hdc: 25 hdc and 8 Popcorns.

Note: Mark Row 2 as **right** side **and** bottom edge.

Row 3: Ch 2, turn; hdc in next st and in each st across: 33 hdc.

Row 4: Ch 2, turn; (hdc in next 3 hdc, work Popcorn in next hdc) across to last 4 hdc, hdc in last 4 hdc: 26 hdc and 7 Popcorns.

Row 5: Ch 2, turn; hdc in next st and in each st across: 33 hdc.

Row 6: Ch 2, turn; hdc in next hdc, work Popcorn in next hdc, (hdc in next 3 hdc, work Popcorn in next hdc) across to last 2 hdc, hdc in last 2 hdc: 25 hdc and 8 Popcorns.

Rows 7-29: Repeat Rows 3-6, 5 times; then repeat Rows 3-5 once **more**.

Finish off.

ASSEMBLY

Using Placement Diagram as a guide and with bottom edges at the same end, sew Panels and Blocks together.

EDGING

Rnd 1: With **right** side facing, join yarn with slip st in any corner; ch 1, ★ 3 sc in corner, work an odd number of sc across to next corner; repeat from ★ around; join with slip st to first sc.

Rnd 2: Slip st in next sc, ch 4 (**counts as first dc plus ch 1**), (dc in same st, ch 1) twice, skip next sc, ★ (dc in next sc, ch 1, skip next sc) across to center sc of next corner, (dc, ch 1) 3 times in center sc, skip next sc; repeat from ★ 2 times **more**, (dc in next sc, ch 1, skip next st) across; join with slip st to first dc.

Rnd 3: Ch 1, sc in same st as joining and in next ch-1 sp, 3 sc in next dc, ★ sc in next ch-1 sp and in each dc and each ch-1 sp across to center dc of next corner, 3 sc in center dc; repeat from ★ 2 times **more**, sc in next ch-1 sp and in each dc and each ch-1 sp across; join with slip st to first sc.

Rnd 4: Ch 1; working from **left** to **right**, work reverse sc in each sc around (*Figs. 3a-d, page 30*); join with slip st to first st, finish off.

PLACEMENT DIAGRAM

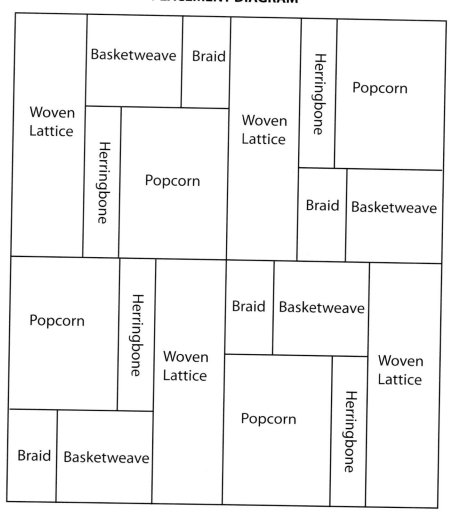

Luck of
the Irish

EASY +

Finished Size: 32½" x 38"
(82.5 cm x 96.5 cm)

SHOPPING LIST

Yarn (Light Weight) 🧶**3**

[3.5 ounces, 254 yards
(100 grams, 232 meters) per skein]:

☐ 6 skeins

Crochet Hook

☐ Size I (5.5 mm)

or size needed for gauge

Additional Supplies

☐ Tapestry needle

GAUGE INFORMATION

14 hdc and 9 rows = 4" (10 cm)

Gauge Swatch: 4" (10 cm) square

Ch 15.

Row 1: Hdc in third ch from hook **(2 skipped chs count as first hdc)** and in each ch across: 14 hdc.

Rows 2-9: Ch 2 **(counts as first hdc)**, turn; hdc in next hdc and in each hdc across.

Finish off.

STITCH GUIDE

BACK POST DOUBLE CROCHET
(abbreviated BPdc)

YO, insert hook from **back** to **front** around post of st indicated *(Fig. 2, page 30)*, YO and pull up a loop (3 loops on hook), (YO and draw through 2 loops on hook) twice.

FRONT POST DOUBLE CROCHET
(abbreviated FPdc)

YO, insert hook from **front** to **back** around post of st indicated *(Fig. 2, page 30)*, YO and pull up a loop (3 loops on hook), (YO and draw through 2 loops on hook) twice.

FRONT POST TREBLE CROCHET
(abbreviated FPtr)

YO twice, insert hook from **front** to **back** around post of st indicated *(Fig. 2, page 30)*, YO and pull up a loop even with loops on hook (4 loops on hook), (YO and draw through 2 loops on hook) 3 times. Skip hdc **behind** FPtr.

FRONT POST DOUBLE TREBLE CROCHET *(abbreviated FPdtr)*

YO 3 times, insert hook from **front** to **back** around post of st indicated *(Fig. 2, page 30)*, YO and pull up a loop even with loops on hook (5 loops on hook), (YO and draw through 2 loops on hook) 4 times. Skip hdc **behind** FPdtr.

POPCORN (uses one hdc)

5 Dc in hdc indicated, drop loop from hook, insert hook in first dc of 5-dc group, hook dropped loop and draw through dc.

DIAMOND PANEL

Finished Size:

10½" wide x 35½" long (26.5 cm x 90 cm)

Ch 36.

Row 1 (Right side)**:** Hdc in third ch from hook **(2 skipped chs count as first hdc)** and in each ch across: 35 hdc.

Note: Loop a short piece of yarn around any stitch to mark Row 1 as **right** side **and** bottom edge.

Row 2: Ch 2 **(counts as first hdc, now and throughout)**, turn; hdc in next hdc and in each hdc across.

Row 3: Ch 2, turn; hdc in next 2 hdc, work FPtr around each of next 2 hdc 2 rows **below**, hdc in next 10 hdc, skip next 3 hdc 2 rows **below**, work FPdtr around each of next 2 hdc 2 rows **below**, hdc in next hdc, working in **front** of last 2 FPdtr made, work FPdtr around each of first 2 skipped hdc 2 rows **below**, hdc in next 10 hdc, work FPtr around each of next 2 hdc 2 rows **below**, hdc in last 3 hdc.

Row 4: Ch 2, turn; hdc in next st and in each st across.

Row 5: Ch 2, turn; hdc in next 2 hdc, work FPtr around each of next 2 FPtr 2 rows **below**, hdc in next 8 hdc, work FPdtr around each of next 2 FPdtr 2 rows **below**, hdc in next 5 hdc, work FPdtr around each of next 2 FPdtr 2 rows **below**, hdc in next 8 hdc, work FPtr around each of next 2 FPtr 2 rows **below**, hdc in last 3 hdc.

Row 6: Ch 2, turn; hdc in next st and in each st across.

Row 7: Ch 2, turn; hdc in next 2 hdc, work FPtr around each of next 2 FPtr 2 rows **below**, hdc in next 6 hdc, work FPdtr around each of next 2 FPdtr 2 rows **below**, hdc in next 9 hdc, work FPdtr around each of next 2 FPdtr 2 rows **below**, hdc in next 6 hdc, work FPtr around each of next 2 FPtr 2 rows **below**, hdc in last 3 hdc.

Row 8: Ch 2, turn; hdc in next st and in each st across.

Row 9: Ch 2, turn; hdc in next 2 hdc, work FPtr around each of next 2 FPtr 2 rows **below**, hdc in next 4 hdc, work FPdtr around each of next 2 FPdtr 2 rows **below**, hdc in next 13 hdc, work FPdtr around each of next 2 FPdtr 2 rows **below**, hdc in next 4 hdc, work FPtr around each of next 2 FPtr 2 rows **below**, hdc in last 3 hdc.

Row 10: Ch 2, turn; hdc in next st and in each st across.

Row 11: Ch 2, turn; hdc in next 2 hdc, work FPtr around each of next 2 FPtr 2 rows **below**, hdc in next 2 hdc, work FPdtr around each of next 2 FPdtr 2 rows **below**, hdc in next 17 hdc, work FPdtr around each of next 2 FPdtr 2 rows **below**, hdc in next 2 hdc, work FPtr around each of next 2 FPtr 2 rows **below**, hdc in last 3 hdc.

Row 12: Ch 2, turn; hdc in next st and in each st across.

Row 13: Ch 2, turn; (hdc in next 2 hdc, work FPtr around each of next 2 FPsts 2 rows **below**) twice, hdc in next 8 hdc, work Popcorn in next hdc, hdc in next 8 hdc, work FPtr around each of next 2 FPdtr 2 rows **below**, hdc in next 2 hdc, work FPtr around each of next 2 FPtr 2 rows **below**, hdc in last 3 hdc.

Row 14: Ch 2, turn; hdc in next st and in each st across.

Row 15: Ch 2, turn; hdc in next 2 hdc, work FPtr around each of next 2 FPtr 2 rows **below**, hdc in next 4 hdc, work FPdtr around each of next 2 FPtr 2 rows **below**, hdc in next 13 hdc, work FPdtr around each of next 2 FPtr 2 rows **below**, hdc in next 4 hdc, work FPtr around each of next 2 FPtr 2 rows **below**, hdc in last 3 hdc.

Row 16: Ch 2, turn; hdc in next st and in each st across.

Row 17: Ch 2, turn; hdc in next 2 hdc, work FPtr around each of next 2 FPtr 2 rows **below**, hdc in next 6 hdc, work FPdtr around each of next 2 FPdtr 2 rows **below**, hdc in next 9 hdc, work FPdtr around each of next 2 FPdtr 2 rows **below**, hdc in next 6 hdc, work FPtr around each of next 2 FPtr 2 rows **below**, hdc in last 3 hdc.

Row 18: Ch 2, turn; hdc in next st and in each st across.

Row 19: Ch 2, turn; hdc in next 2 hdc, work FPtr around each of next 2 FPtr 2 rows **below**, hdc in next 8 hdc, work FPdtr around each of next 2 FPdtr 2 rows **below**, hdc in next 5 hdc, work FPdtr around each of next 2 FPdtr 2 rows **below**, hdc in next 8 hdc, work FPtr around each of next 2 FPtr 2 rows **below**, hdc in last 3 hdc.

Row 20: Ch 2, turn; hdc in next st and in each st across.

Row 21: Ch 2, turn; hdc in next 2 hdc, work FPtr around each of next 2 FPtr 2 rows **below**, hdc in next 10 hdc, work FPdtr around each of next 2 FPdtr 2 rows **below**, hdc in next hdc, work FPdtr around each of next 2 FPdtr 2 rows **below**, hdc in next 10 hdc, work FPtr around each of next 2 FPtr 2 rows **below**, hdc in last 3 hdc.

Row 22: Ch 2, turn; hdc in next st and in each st across.

Row 23: Ch 2, turn; hdc in next 2 hdc, work FPtr around each of next 2 FPtr 2 rows **below**, hdc in next 10 hdc, skip next 2 FPdtr 2 rows **below**, work FPdtr around each of next 2 FPdtr 2 rows **below**, hdc in next hdc, working in **front** of last 2 FPdtr made, work FPdtr around each of 2 skipped FPdtr 2 rows **below**, hdc in next 10 hdc, work FPtr around each of next 2 FPtr 2 rows **below**, hdc in last 3 hdc.

Row 24: Ch 2, turn; hdc in next st and in each st across.

Rows 25-84: Repeat Rows 5-24, 3 times.

Finish off.

BASKETWEAVE PANEL
(Make 2)
Finished Size: 9¾" wide x 35½" long (25 cm x 90 cm)

Ch 40.

Row 1 (Right side)**:** Dc in fourth ch from hook (**3 skipped chs count as first dc**) and in each ch across: 38 dc.

Note: Mark Row 1 as **right** side **and** bottom edge.

Row 2: Ch 2, turn; work BPdc around each of next 4 dc, ★ work FPdc around each of next 4 dc, work BPdc around each of next 4 dc; repeat from ★ across to last dc, hdc in last dc.

Rows 3 and 4: Ch 2, turn; work FPdc around each of next 4 sts, ★ work BPdc around each of next 4 sts, work FPdc around each of next 4 sts; repeat from ★ across to last hdc, hdc in last hdc.

Rows 5 and 6: Ch 2, turn; work BPdc around each of next 4 sts, ★ work FPdc around each of next 4 sts, work BPdc around each of next 4 sts; repeat from ★ across to last hdc, hdc in last hdc.

Repeat Rows 3-6 for pattern until piece measures same as Diamond Panel, ending by working Row 3.

Finish off.

ASSEMBLY
With bottom edges at the same end and placing Diamond Panel in the center, sew Panels together.

EDGING
Rnd 1: With **right** side facing, join yarn with slip st in any corner; ch 1, ★ 3 sc in corner, work an odd number of sc across to next corner; repeat from ★ around; join with slip st to first sc.

Rnd 2: Slip st in next sc, ch 4 (**counts as first dc plus ch 1**), (dc in same st, ch 1) twice, skip next sc, ★ (dc in next sc, ch 1, skip next sc) across to center sc of next corner, (dc, ch 1) 3 times in center sc, skip next sc; repeat from ★ 2 times **more**, (dc in next sc, ch 1, skip next st) across; join with slip st to first dc.

Rnd 3: Slip st in next ch-1 sp, ch 1, (sc, ch 3, slip st in third ch from hook, sc) in same ch-1 sp and in each ch-1 sp around; join with slip st to first sc, finish off.

Staghorn

EASY +

Finished Size: 30½" x 30"
(77.5 cm x 76 cm)

SHOPPING LIST
Yarn (Light Weight)
**[3.5 ounces, 254 yards
(100 grams, 232 meters) per skein]:**
☐ 4 skeins

Crochet Hook
☐ Size I (5.5 mm)
> **or** size needed for gauge

Additional Supplies
☐ Tapestry needle

GAUGE INFORMATION

In pattern, 10 sts = 3" (7.5 cm);
   14 rows = 5" (12.75 cm)

Gauge Swatch: 4¼" wide x 5" high
   (10.75 cm x 12.75 cm)

Ch 15.

Row 1: Hdc in third ch from hook
(2 skipped chs count as first hdc)
and in each ch across: 14 hdc.

Rows 2-14: Ch 2 **(counts as first
hdc)**, turn; hdc in next hdc and in
each hdc across.

Finish off.

STITCH GUIDE

FRONT POST TREBLE CROCHET
(abbreviated FPtr)
YO twice, insert hook from **front**
to **back** around post of st
indicated *(Fig. 2, page 30)*, YO and
pull up a loop even with loops on
hook (4 loops on hook), (YO and
draw through 2 loops on hook) 3
times. Skip hdc **behind** FPtr.

**FRONT POST DOUBLE TREBLE
CROCHET** *(abbreviated FPdtr)*
YO 3 times, insert hook from **front**
to **back** around post of st
indicated *(Fig. 2, page 30)*, YO and
pull up a loop even with loops on
hook (5 loops on hook), (YO and
draw through 2 loops on hook) 4
times. Skip hdc **behind** FPdtr.

BODY

Ch 101.

Row 1 (Right side)**:** Hdc in third ch
from hook **(2 skipped chs count
as first hdc)** and in each ch across:
100 hdc.

Row 2: Ch 2 **(counts as first hdc,
now and throughout)**, turn; hdc in
next hdc and in each hdc across.

Row 3: Ch 2, turn; hdc in next hdc,
† work FPtr around each of next
2 hdc 2 rows **below**, hdc in next
8 hdc, work FPtr around each of
next 4 hdc 2 rows **below**, hdc in next
8 hdc, work FPtr around each of next
2 hdc 2 rows **below** †, hdc in next
48 hdc, repeat from † to † once, hdc
in last 2 hdc.

Row 4: Ch 2, turn; hdc in next st and
in each st across.

Row 5: Ch 2, turn; hdc in next hdc,
† work FPtr around each of next
2 FPtr 2 rows **below**, hdc in next
6 hdc, work FPdtr around each of
next 2 FPtr 2 rows **below**, hdc in next
4 hdc, work FPdtr around each of
next 2 FPtr 2 rows **below**, hdc in next
6 hdc, work FPtr around each of next
2 FPtr 2 rows **below** †, hdc in next
48 hdc, repeat from † to † once, hdc
in last 2 hdc.

Row 6: Ch 2, turn; hdc in next st and
in each st across.

Row 7: Ch 2, turn; hdc in next hdc,
† work FPtr around each of next
2 FPtr 2 rows **below**, hdc in next
4 hdc, work FPdtr around each of
next 2 FPdtr 2 rows **below**, hdc in
next 8 hdc, work FPdtr around each
of next 2 FPdtr 2 rows **below**, hdc in
next 4 hdc, work FPtr around each
of next 2 FPtr 2 rows **below** †, hdc in
next 48 hdc, repeat from † to † once,
hdc in last 2 hdc.

Row 8: Ch 2, turn; hdc in next st and
in each st across.

Row 9: Ch 2, turn; hdc in next hdc,
† work FPtr around each of next
2 FPtr 2 rows **below**, hdc in next
2 hdc, work FPdtr around each of
next 2 FPdtr 2 rows **below**, hdc in
next 4 hdc, work FPtr around each
of next 4 hdc 2 rows **below**, hdc in
next 4 hdc, work FPdtr around each
of next 2 FPdtr 2 rows **below**, hdc in
next 2 hdc, work FPtr around each
of next 2 FPtr 2 rows **below** †, hdc in
next 48 hdc, repeat from † to † once,
hdc in last 2 hdc.

Rows 10-32: Repeat Rows 4-9,
3 times; then repeat Rows 4-8 once
more.

Row 33 (seat belt opening): Ch 2, turn; hdc in next hdc, † work FPtr around each of next 2 FPtr 2 rows **below**, hdc in next 2 hdc, work FPdtr around each of next 2 FPdtr 2 rows **below**, hdc in next 4 hdc, work FPtr around each of next 4 hdc 2 rows **below**, hdc in next 4 hdc, work FPdtr around each of next 2 FPdtr 2 rows **below**, hdc in next 2 hdc, work FPtr around each of next 2 FPtr 2 rows **below** †, hdc in next 17 hdc, ch 14, skip next 14 hdc, hdc in next 17 hdc, repeat from † to † once, hdc in last 2 hdc: 86 sts and one ch-14 sp.

Row 34: Ch 2, turn; hdc in next st and in each st across working 14 hdc in ch-14 sp: 100 hdc.

Rows 35-56: Repeat Rows 5-9 once, then repeat Rows 4-9 twice, then repeat Rows 4-8 once **more**.

Rows 57-80: Repeat Rows 33-56.

Row 81: Ch 2, turn; hdc in next hdc, † work FPtr around each of next 2 FPtr 2 rows **below**, hdc in next 2 hdc, work FPdtr around each of next 2 FPdtr 2 rows **below**, hdc in next 12 hdc, work FPdtr around each of next 2 FPdtr 2 rows **below**, hdc in next 2 hdc, work FPtr around each of next 2 FPtr 2 rows **below** †, hdc in next 48 hdc, repeat from † to † once, hdc in last 2 hdc.

Row 82: Ch 2, turn; hdc in next st and in each st across; do **not** finish off.

EDGING

Rnd 1: Ch 1, turn; sc evenly around entire Body working 3 sc in each corner; join with slip st to first sc.

Rnd 2: Ch 1; working from **left** to **right**, work reverse sc in each sc around *(Figs. 3a-d, page 30)*; join with slip st to first st, finish off.

Squares

 **EASY +**

Finished Size: 34" (86.5 cm) square

SHOPPING LIST

Yarn (Light Weight)

[3.5 ounces, 254 yards
(100 grams, 232 meters) per skein]:

☐ 5 skeins

Crochet Hook

☐ Size I (5.5 mm)

  or size needed for gauge

Additional Supplies

☐ Tapestry needle

GAUGE INFORMATON

In pattern,

   14 sts and 10 rows = 4" (10 cm)

Gauge Swatch: 8¼" (21 cm) square
Work same as Square.

STITCH GUIDE

FRONT POST TREBLE CROCHET
(abbreviated FPtr)
YO twice, insert hook from **front**
to **back** around post of st
indicated *(Fig. 2, page 30)*, YO and
pull up a loop even with loops on
hook (4 loops on hook), (YO and
draw through 2 loops on hook) 3
times. Skip hdc **behind** FPtr.

POPCORN (uses one hdc)
5 Dc in hdc indicated, drop loop
from hook, insert hook in first dc
of 5-dc group, hook dropped loop
and draw through dc.

SQUARE (Make 16)

Ch 30.

Row 1 (Right side)**:** Hdc in third ch
from hook (**2 skipped chs count as
first hdc**) and in each ch across: 29 hdc.

Note: Loop a short piece of yarn
around any stitch to mark Row 1 as
right side.

Row 2: Ch 2 (**counts as first hdc,
now and throughout**), turn; hdc in
next hdc and in each hdc across.

Row 3: Ch 2, turn; hdc in next hdc,
work FPtr around hdc one row **below**
next hdc, ★ hdc in next 3 hdc, work
FPtr around hdc one row **below** next
hdc; repeat from ★ across to last 2 hdc,
hdc in last 2 hdc: 22 hdc and 7 FPtr.

Row 4: Ch 2, turn; hdc in next st and
in each st across: 29 hdc.

Row 5: Ch 2, turn; hdc in next hdc,
work FPtr around FPtr 2 rows **below**,
★ hdc in next hdc, work Popcorn in
next hdc, hdc in next hdc, work FPtr
around FPtr 2 rows **below**; repeat
from ★ across to last 2 hdc, hdc in last
2 hdc: 16 hdc, 7 FPtr and 6 Popcorns.

Row 6: Ch 2, turn; hdc in next st and
in each st across: 29 hdc.

Row 7: Ch 2, turn; hdc in next hdc,
work FPtr around FPtr 2 rows **below**,
★ hdc in next 3 hdc, work FPtr
around FPtr 2 rows **below**; repeat
from ★ across to last 2 hdc, hdc in
last 2 hdc: 22 hdc and 7 FPtr.

Rows 8-19: Repeat Rows 4-7, 3 times.

Rows 20 and 21: Repeat Rows 6
and 7.

Finish off leaving a long end for
sewing.

ASSEMBLY

With **wrong** sides together, using
photo, page 20, as a guide for
placement and alternating the
direction of Squares as shown,
whipstitch Squares together *(Fig. A)*,
forming 4 vertical strips of 4 Squares
each, beginning and ending in
corners; then whipstitch strips
together in same manner.

Fig. A

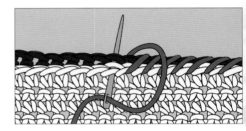

EDGING

Rnd 1: With **right** side facing, join
yarn with slip st in any corner; ch 1, sc
evenly around entire piece working
3 sc in each corner; join with slip st to
first sc.

Rnd 2: Ch 1, sc in each sc around
working 3 sc in center sc of each
corner; join with slip st to first sc.

Rnd 3: Ch 1; working from **left** to
right, work reverse sc in each sc
around *(Figs. 3a-d, page 30)*; join
with slip st to first st, finish off.

Popcorn & Lattice

EASY +

Finished Size: 41" x 41½"
    (104 cm x 105.5 cm)

SHOPPING LIST

Yarn (Light Weight)
[5 ounces, 459 yards
(140 grams, 420 meters) per skein]:
- ❏ 5 skeins

Crochet Hook
- ❏ Size G (4 mm)
    or size needed for gauge

Additional Supplies
- ❏ Tapestry needle

GAUGE INFORMATION

16 hdc = 4" (10 cm);

   14 rows = 5" (10.75 cm)

Gauge Swatch: 4" wide x 5" high (10 cm x 12.75 cm)

Ch 17.

Row 1: Hdc in third ch from hook (**2 skipped chs count as first hdc**) and in each ch across: 16 hdc.

Rows 2-14: Ch 2 (**counts as first hdc**), turn; hdc in next hdc and in each hdc across.

Finish off.

STITCH GUIDE

FRONT POST TREBLE CROCHET

   (abbreviated FPtr)

YO twice, insert hook from **front** to **back** around post of st indicated *(Fig. 2, page 30)*, YO and pull up a loop even with loops on hook (4 loops on hook), (YO and draw through 2 loops on hook) 3 times. Skip hdc **behind** FPtr.

FRONT POST DOUBLE TREBLE CROCHET

   (abbreviated FPdtr)

YO 3 times, insert hook from **front** to **back** around post of st indicated *(Fig. 2, page 30)*, YO and pull up a loop even with loops on hook (5 loops on hook), (YO and draw through 2 loops on hook) 4 times. Skip hdc **behind** FPdtr.

POPCORN (uses one hdc)

5 Dc in hdc indicated, drop loop from hook, insert hook in first dc of 5-dc group, hook dropped loop and draw through dc.

LATTICE PANEL (Make 2)

Finished Size: 12¾" wide x 41" long
(32.5 cm x 104 cm)

Ch 52.

Row 1 (Right side)**:** Hdc in third ch from hook (**2 skipped chs count as first hdc, now and throughout**) and in each ch across: 51 hdc.

Note: Loop a short piece of yarn around any stitch to mark Row 1 as **right** side **and** bottom edge.

Row 2: Ch 2 (**counts as first hdc, now and throughout**), turn; hdc in next hdc and in each hdc across.

Row 3: Ch 2, turn; hdc in next hdc, work FPtr around each of next 2 hdc 2 rows **below**, hdc in next 4 hdc, work FPtr around each of next 2 hdc 2 rows **below**, hdc in next hdc, work FPtr around each of next 2 hdc 2 rows **below**, ★ hdc in next 5 hdc, work FPtr around each of next 2 hdc 2 rows **below**, hdc in next hdc, work FPtr around each of next 2 hdc 2 rows **below**; repeat from ★ 2 times **more**, hdc in next 4 hdc, work FPtr around each of next 2 hdc 2 rows **below**, hdc in last 2 hdc.

Row 4: Ch 2, turn; hdc in next st and in each st across.

Row 5: Ch 2, turn; hdc in next hdc, work FPtr around each of next 2 FPtr 2 rows **below**, hdc in next 4 hdc, skip next 2 FPsts 2 rows **below**, work FPdtr around each of next 2 FPsts rows **below**, hdc in next hdc, working in **front** of last 2 FPdtr made, work FPdtr around each of 2 skipped FPsts 2 rows **below**, ★ hdc in next 5 hdc, skip next 2 FPsts 2 rows **below**, work FPdtr around each of next 2 FPsts rows **below**, hdc in next hdc, working in **front** of last 2 FPdtr made, work FPdtr around each of 2 skipped FPsts 2 rows **below**; repeat from ★ 2 times **more**, hdc in next 4 hdc, work FPtr around each of next 2 FPtr 2 rows **below**, hdc in last 2 hdc.

Row 6: Ch 2, turn; hdc in next st and in each st across.

Row 7: Ch 2, turn; hdc in next hdc, work FPtr around each of next 2 FPtr 2 rows **below**, hdc in next 2 hdc, work FPdtr around each of next 2 FPdtr 2 rows **below**, hdc in next 5 hdc, work FPdtr around each of next 2 FPdtr 2 rows **below**, ★ hdc in next hdc, work FPdtr around each of next 2 FPdtr 2 rows **below**, hdc in next 5 hdc, work FPdtr around each of next 2 FPdtr 2 rows **below**; repeat from ★ 2 times **more**, hdc in next 2 hdc, work FPtr around each of next 2 FPtr 2 rows **below**, hdc in last 2 hdc.

Row 8: Ch 2, turn; hdc in next st and in each st across.

Row 9: Ch 2, turn; hdc in next hdc, work FPtr around each of next 2 FPtr 2 rows **below**, hdc in next 2 hdc, work FPtr around each of next 2 FPsts 2 rows **below**, hdc in next 5 hdc, ★ skip next 2 FPsts 2 rows **below**, work FPdtr around each of next 2 FPsts rows **below**, hdc in next hdc, working **behind** last 2 FPdtr made, work FPdtr around each of 2 skipped FPsts 2 rows **below**, hdc in next 5 hdc; repeat from ★ 2 times **more**, (work FPtr around each of next 2 FPsts 2 rows **below**, hdc in next 2 hdc) twice.

Row 10: Ch 2, turn; hdc in next st and in each st across.

Row 11: Ch 2, turn; hdc in next hdc, work FPtr around each of next 2 FPtr 2 rows **below**, hdc in next 2 hdc, work FPtr around each of next 2 FPtr 2 rows **below**, hdc in next 5 hdc, work FPtr around each of next 2 FPdtr 2 rows **below**, ★ hdc in next hdc, work FPtr around each of next 2 FPdtr 2 rows **below**, hdc in next 5 hdc, work FPtr around each of next 2 FPsts 2 rows **below**; repeat from ★ 2 times **more**, hdc in next 2 hdc, work FPtr around each of next 2 FPtr 2 rows **below**, hdc in last 2 hdc.

Row 12: Ch 2, turn; hdc in next st and in each st across.

Rows 13 and 14: Repeat Rows 9 and 10.

Row 15: Ch 2, turn; hdc in next hdc, work FPtr around each of next 2 FPtr 2 rows **below**, hdc in next 4 hdc, work FPdtr around each of next 2 FPsts 2 rows **below**, hdc in next hdc, work FPdtr around each of next 2 FPsts 2 rows **below**, ★ hdc in next 5 hdc, work FPdtr around each of next 2 FPsts 2 rows **below**, hdc in next hdc, work FPdtr around each of next 2 FPsts 2 rows **below**; repeat from ★ 2 times **more**, hdc in next 4 hdc, work FPtr around each of next 2 FPtr 2 rows **below**, hdc in last 2 hdc.

Row 16: Ch 2, turn; hdc in next st and in each st across.

Rows 17 and 18: Repeat Rows 5 and 6.

Row 19: Ch 2, turn; hdc in next hdc, work FPtr around each of next 2 FPtr 2 rows **below**, hdc in next 4 hdc, work FPdtr around each of next 2 FPdtr 2 rows **below**, hdc in next hdc, work FPtr around each of next 2 FPdtr 2 rows **below**, ★ hdc in next 5 hdc, work FPtr around each of next 2 FPdtr 2 rows **below**, hdc in next hdc, work FPtr around each of next 2 FPdtr 2 rows **below**; repeat from ★ 2 times **more**, hdc in next 4 hdc, work FPtr around each of next 2 FPtr 2 rows **below**, hdc in last 2 hdc.

Rows 20-115: Repeat Rows 4-19, 6 times.

Finish off.

POPCORN PANEL

Finished Size: 15¼" wide x 41" long (39 cm x 104 cm)

Ch 62.

Row 1: Hdc in third ch from hook and in each ch across: 61 hdc.

Row 2 (Right side)**:** Ch 2, turn; hdc in next hdc, work Popcorn in next hdc, (hdc in next 3 hdc, work Popcorn in next hdc) across to last 2 hdc, hdc in last 2 hdc: 46 hdc and 15 Popcorns.

Note: Mark Row 2 as **right** side **and** bottom edge.

Row 3: Ch 2, turn; hdc in next st and in each st across: 61 hdc.

Row 4: Ch 2, turn; (hdc in next 3 hdc, work Popcorn in next hdc) across to last 4 hdc, hdc in last 4 hdc: 47 hdc and 14 Popcorns.

Row 5: Ch 2, turn; hdc in next st and in each st across: 61 hdc.

Row 6: Ch 2, turn; hdc in next hdc, work Popcorn in next hdc, (hdc in next 3 hdc, work Popcorn in next hdc) across to last 2 hdc, hdc in last 2 hdc: 46 hdc and 15 Popcorns.

Repeat Rows 3-6 for pattern until piece measures same as Lattice Panel, ending by working a **wrong** side row.

Finish off.

ASSEMBLY

With bottom edges at the same end and placing Popcorn Panel in the center, sew Panels together.

EDGING

Rnd 1: With **right** side facing, join yarn with slip st in any corner; ch 1, sc evenly around entire piece working 3 sc in each corner; join with slip st to first sc.

Rnd 2: Ch 1; working from **left** to **right**, work reverse sc in each sc around *(Figs. 3a-d, page 30)*; join with slip st to first st, finish off.

TASSEL (Make 4)

Cut a piece of cardboard 6" (15 cm) square. Wind a double strand of yarn around the cardboard approximately 19 times. Cut an 18" (45.5 cm) length of yarn and insert it under all of the strands at the top of the cardboard; pull up **tightly** and tie securely. Leave the yarn ends long enough to attach the tassel. Cut the yarn at the opposite end of the cardboard and then remove it *(Fig. A)*. Cut a 12" (30.5 cm) length of yarn and wrap it tightly around the tassel several times, 1" (2.5 cm) below the top *(Fig. B)*; tie securely. Trim the ends. Sew one Tassel to each corner of piece.

Fig. A

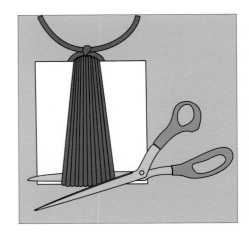

Fig. B

General Instructions

ABBREVIATIONS

BPdc	Back Post double crochet(s)
ch(s)	chain(s)
cm	centimeters
dc	double crochet(s)
FPdc	Front Post double crochet(s)
FPdtr	Front Post double treble crochet(s)
FPst(s)	Front Post stitch(es)
FPtr	Front Post treble crochet(s)
hdc	half double crochet(s)
mm	millimeters
Rnd(s)	Round(s)
sc	single crochet(s)
st(s)	stitch(es)
YO	yarn over

SYMBOLS & TERMS

★ — work instructions following ★ as many **more** times as indicated in addition to the first time.

† to † — work all instructions from first † to second † **as many** times as specified.

( ) or [ ] — work enclosed instructions **as many** times as specified by the number immediately following **or** work all enclosed instructions in the stitch or space indicated **or** contains explanatory remarks.

colon (:) — the number(s) given after a colon at the end of a row or round denotes the number of stitches or spaces you should have on that row or round.

CROCHET TERMINOLOGY

UNITED STATES		INTERNATIONAL
slip stitch (slip st)	=	single crochet (sc)
single crochet (sc)	=	double crochet (dc)
half double crochet (hdc)	=	half treble crochet (htr)
double crochet (dc)	=	treble crochet (tr)
treble crochet (tr)	=	double treble crochet (dtr)
double treble crochet (dtr)	=	triple treble crochet (ttr)
triple treble crochet (tr tr)	=	quadruple treble crochet (qtr)
skip	=	miss

GAUGE

Exact gauge is **essential** for proper size. Before beginning your project, make the sample swatch given in the individual instructions in the yarn and hook specified. After completing the swatch, measure it, counting your stitches and rows/rounds carefully. If your swatch is larger or smaller than specified, **make another, changing hook size to get the correct gauge**. Keep trying until you find the size hook that will give you the specified gauge.

CROCHET HOOKS																
U.S.	B-1	C-2	D-3	E-4	F-5	G-6	7	H-8	I-9	J-10	K-10½	L-11	M/N-13	N/P-15	P/Q	Q	S
Metric - mm	2.25	2.75	3.25	3.5	3.75	4	4.5	5	5.5	6	6.5	8	9	10	15	16	19

■□□□ **BEGINNER**	Projects for first-time crocheters using basic stitches. Minimal shaping.
■■□□ **EASY**	Projects using yarn with basic stitches, repetitive stitch patterns, simple color changes, and simple shaping and finishing.
■■■□ **INTERMEDIATE**	Projects using a variety of techniques, such as basic lace patterns or color patterns, mid-level shaping and finishing.
■■■■ **EXPERIENCED**	Projects with intricate stitch patterns, techniques and dimension, such as non-repeating patterns, multi-color techniques, fine threads, small hooks, detailed shaping and refined finishing.

BACK RIDGE

Work only in loops indicated by arrows (*Fig. 1*).

Fig. 1

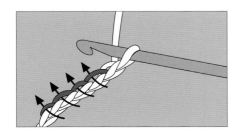

POST STITCH

Work around post of stitch indicated, insert hook in direction of arrow (*Fig. 2*).

Fig. 2

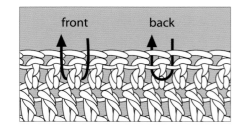

REVERSE SINGLE CROCHET
(abbreviated reverse sc)

Working from **left** to **right**, ★ insert hook in stitch to right of hook (*Fig. 3a*), YO and draw through, under and to left of loop on hook (2 loops on hook) (*Fig. 3b*), YO and draw through both loops on hook (*Fig. 3c*) (**reverse sc made,** *Fig. 3d*); repeat from ★ around.

Fig. 3a

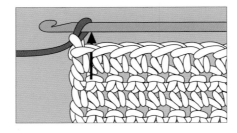

Fig. 3b

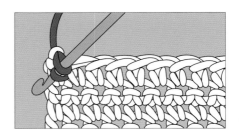

Fig. 3c

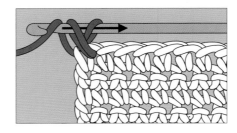

Fig. 3d

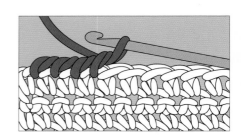

Yarn Weight Symbol & Names	LACE 0	SUPER FINE 1	FINE 2	LIGHT 3	MEDIUM 4	BULKY 5	SUPER BULKY 6	JUMBO 7
Type of Yarns in Category	Fingering, size 10 crochet thread	Sock, Fingering, Baby	Sport, Baby	DK, Light Worsted	Worsted, Afghan, Aran	Chunky, Craft, Rug	Super Bulky, Roving	Jumbo, Roving
Crochet Gauge* Ranges in Single Crochet to 4" (10 cm)	32-42 sts**	21-32 sts	16-20 sts	12-17 sts	11-14 sts	8-11 sts	6-9 sts	5 sts and fewer
Advised Hook Size Range	Steel*** 6 to 8, Regular hook B-1	B-1 to E-4	E-4 to 7	7 to I-9	I-9 to K-10½	K-10½ to M/N-13	M/N-13 to Q	Q and larger

*GUIDELINES ONLY: The chart above reflects the most commonly used gauges and hook sizes for specific yarn categories.

** Lace weight yarns are usually crocheted with larger hooks to create lacy openwork patterns. Accordingly, a gauge range is difficult to determine. Always follow the gauge stated in your pattern.

*** Steel crochet hooks are sized differently from regular hooks–the higher the number, the smaller the hook, which is the reverse of regular hook sizing.

Yarn Information

The Blankets in this book were made using Light Weight Yarn. Any brand of Light Weight Yarn may be used. It is best to refer to the yardage/meters when determining how many balls or skeins to purchase. Remember, to arrive at the finished size, it is the GAUGE/TENSION that is important, not the brand of yarn.

For your convenience, listed below are the yarn styles and colors used to create our photography models. Because yarn manufacturers make frequent changes in their product lines, you may sometimes find it necessary to use a substitute yarn or to search for the discontinued product at alternate suppliers (locally or online).

CABLES

Lion Brand® Vanna's Style

#174 Olive

LUCK OF THE IRISH

Lion Brand® Vanna's Style

#178 Teal

SQUARES

Lion Brand® Vanna's Style

#149 Silver

HEIRLOOM

Lion Brand® Vanna's Style

#098 Ecru

STAGHORN

Lion Brand® Vanna's Style

#134 Tomato

POPCORN & LATTICE

Lion Brand® Baby Soft®

#170 Pistachio

MELISSA LEAPMAN

With more than 800 knit and crochet designs in print, Melissa Leapman is one of the most widely published American designers working today.

She began her design career by freelancing for leading ready-to-wear design houses in New York City. She also created designs to help top yarn companies promote their new and existing yarns each season. Her ability to quickly develop fully envisioned garments put her skills in great demand.

Through the years, Leisure Arts has published more than 40 books of Melissa's fabulous designs. Melissa is also the host of several Leisure Arts DVDs in the best-selling teach-yourself series, "I Can't Believe I'm Knitting" and "I Can't Believe I'm Crocheting."

Nationally, her designs have been featured in numerous magazines, and her workshops on knitting and crochet are consistently popular with crafters of all skill levels. She has taught at major events such as STITCHES, Vogue Knitting LIVE, and The Knitting Guild Association conferences, as well as at hundreds of yarn shops and local guild events across the country.

To find more of Melissa's designs, visit LeisureArts.com, Melissa's Facebook page, and Ravelry.com.

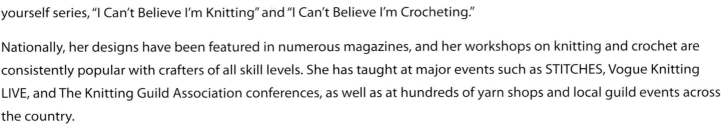

We have made every effort to ensure that these instructions are accurate and complete. We cannot, however, be responsible for human error, typographical mistakes, or variations in individual work.

Production Team: Instructional/Technical Editor - Linda A. Daley; Editorial Writer - Susan Frantz Wiles; Senior Graphic Artist - Lora Puls; Graphic Artist - Kellie McAnulty; Photo Stylist - Lori Wenger; and Photographer - Jason Masters.